ENTER THE DRAGON

SCRAPBOOK SEQUENCES VOLUME 12 PART 2

INTRODUCTION

In an era before the digital age, these images are not just snapshots frozen in time; they are windows into the dedication, passion, and unparalleled charisma that Bruce Lee brought to every frame. As we leaf through these pages, we witness the meticulous choreography of fight sequences, the camaraderie among the cast and crew, and the intense focus that Lee brought to each scene.

"Enter the Dragon" holds a unique place in the history of cinema, not only for its ground-breaking martial arts sequences but also for its cultural impact. Bruce Lee's magnetic presence transcended borders and connected with audiences on a profound level. This collection of behind-the-scenes photographs allows us to witness the man behind the legend—the moments of laughter, the intensity of concentration, and the genuine bonds forged during the making of this cinematic gem.

As we navigate through the candid shots and carefully curated images, it becomes evident that "Bruce Lee On Set" is not just a celebration of a film but a tribute to the man who revolutionized martial arts on screen. The photographs speak a language of their own, conveying the spirit of a cultural icon who left an indelible mark on the world.

We extend our gratitude to the photographers who skilfully captured these moments, freezing them in time for us to savour. This photo book is a testament to the enduring legacy of Bruce Lee and the timeless magic that unfolds when passion, talent, and dedication converge on a film set.

Thank you for embarking on this visual journey through the lens of history, where Bruce Lee's spirit lives on in every frame.

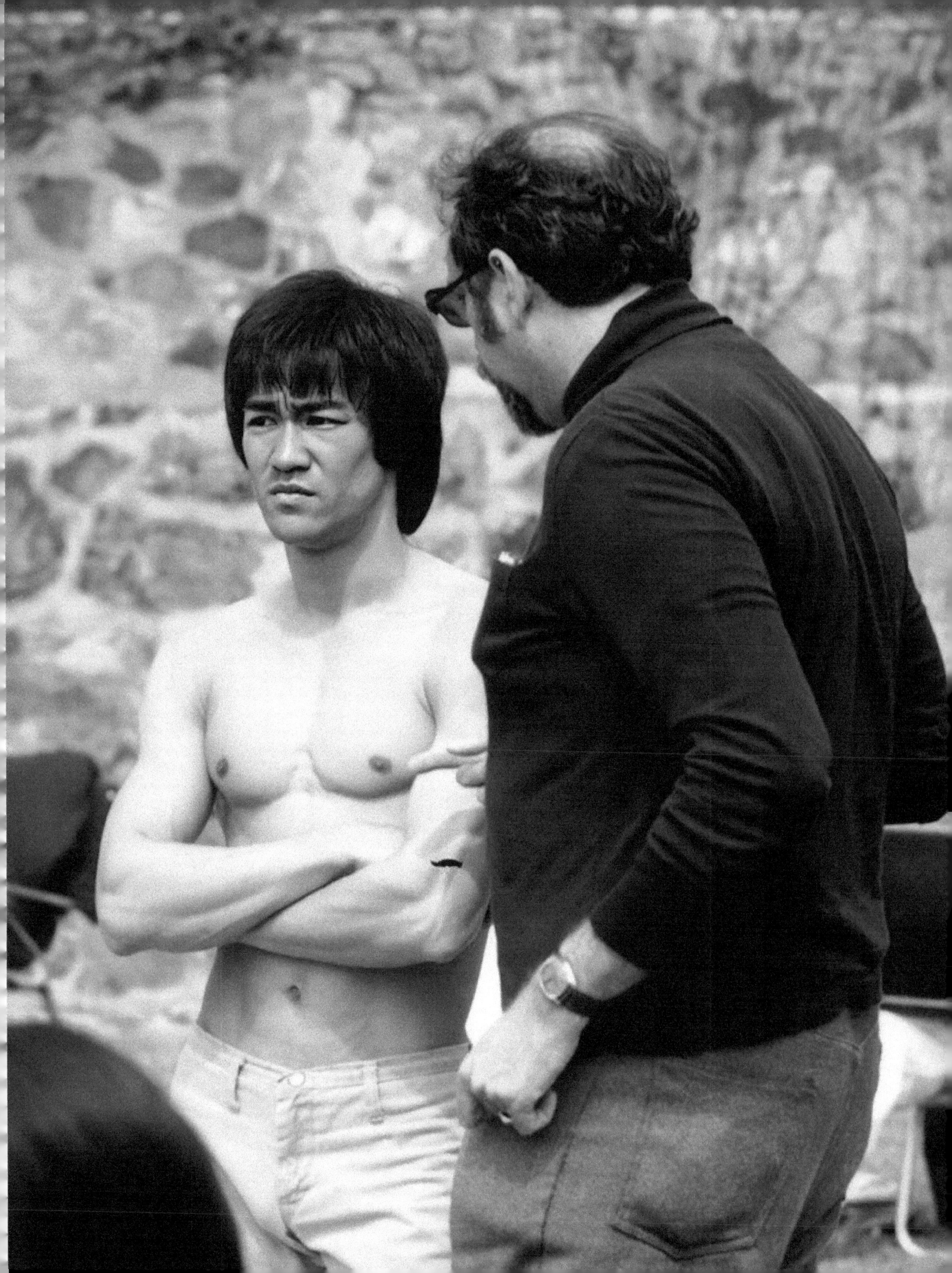

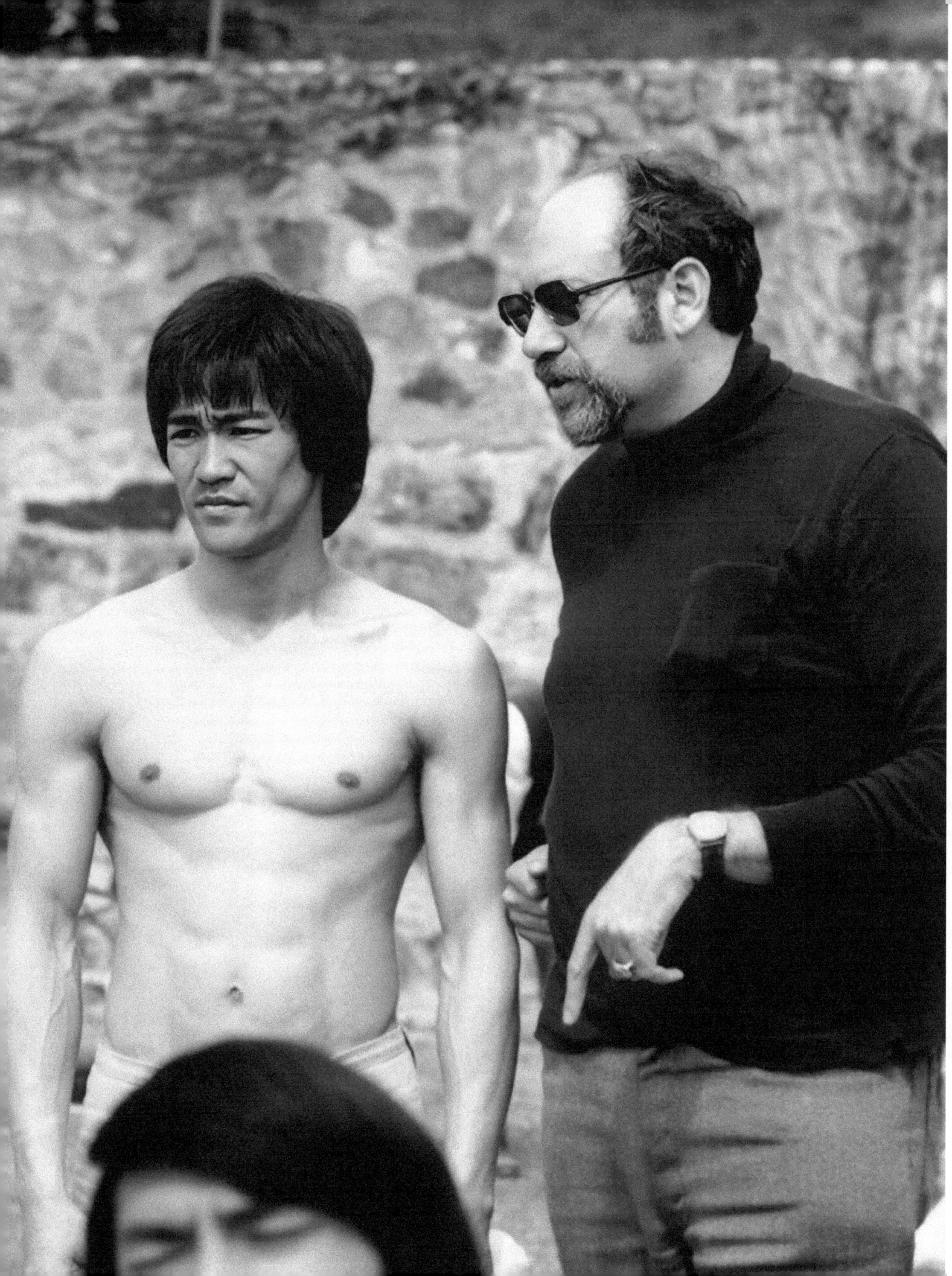

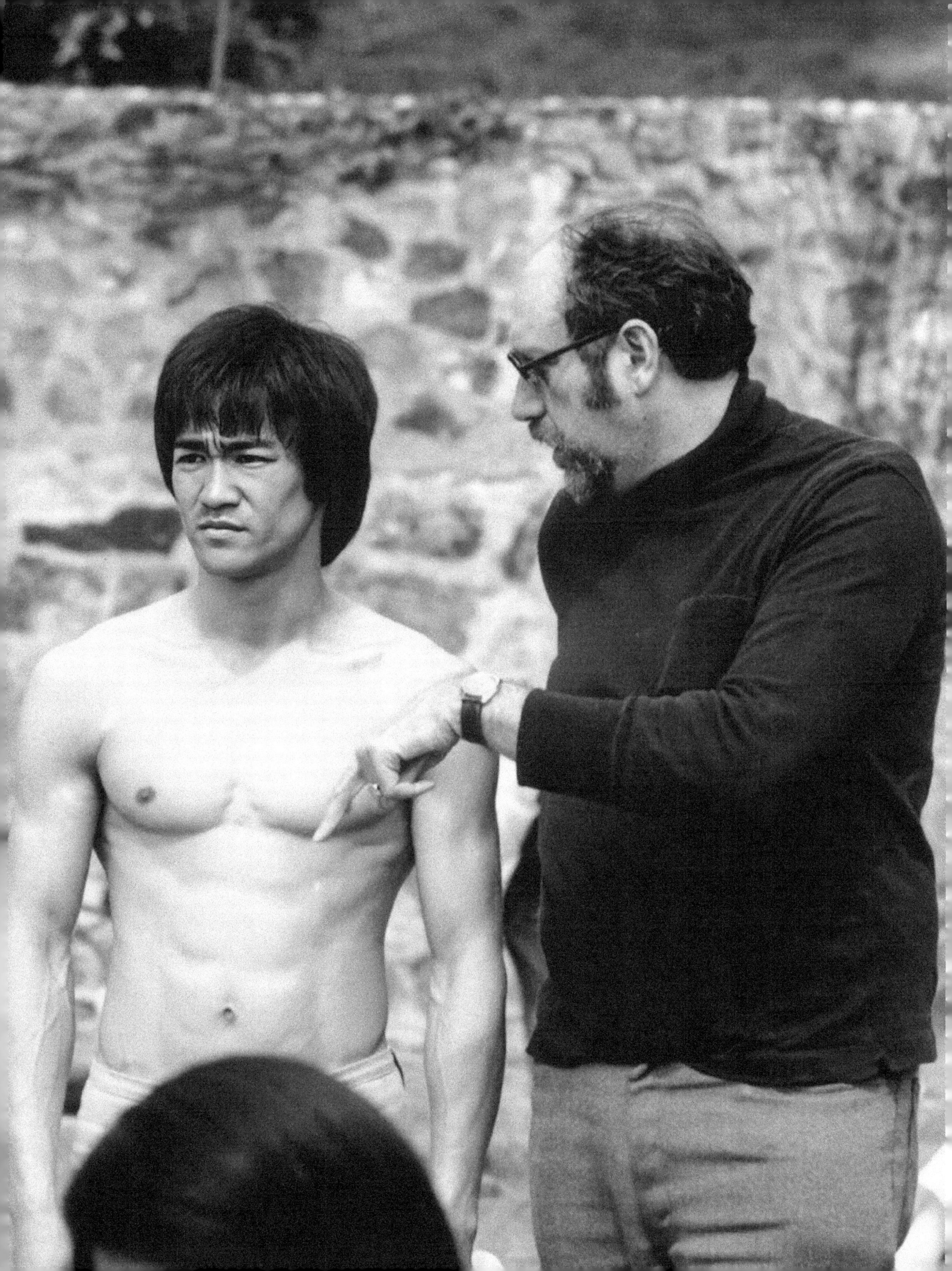

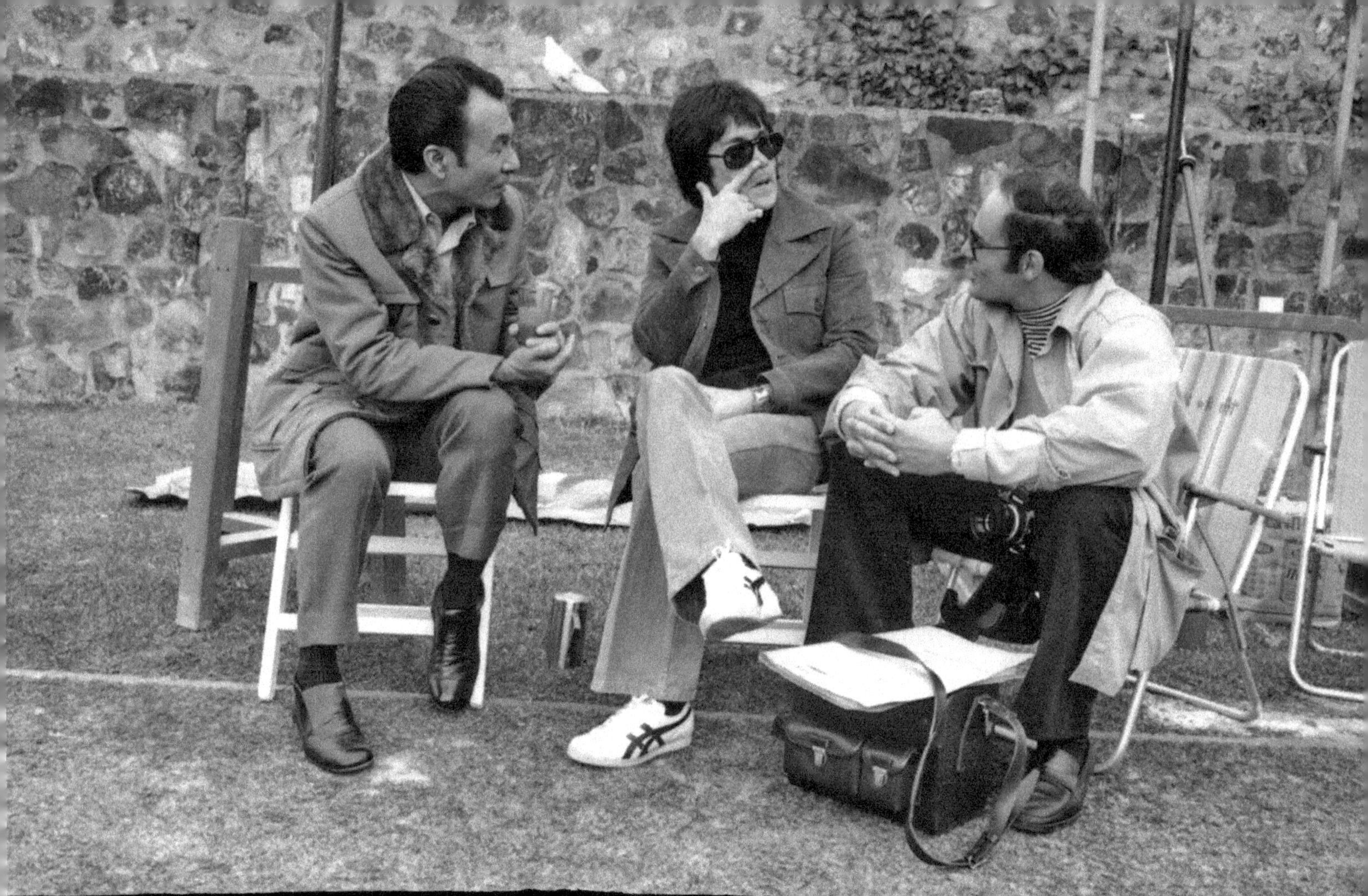

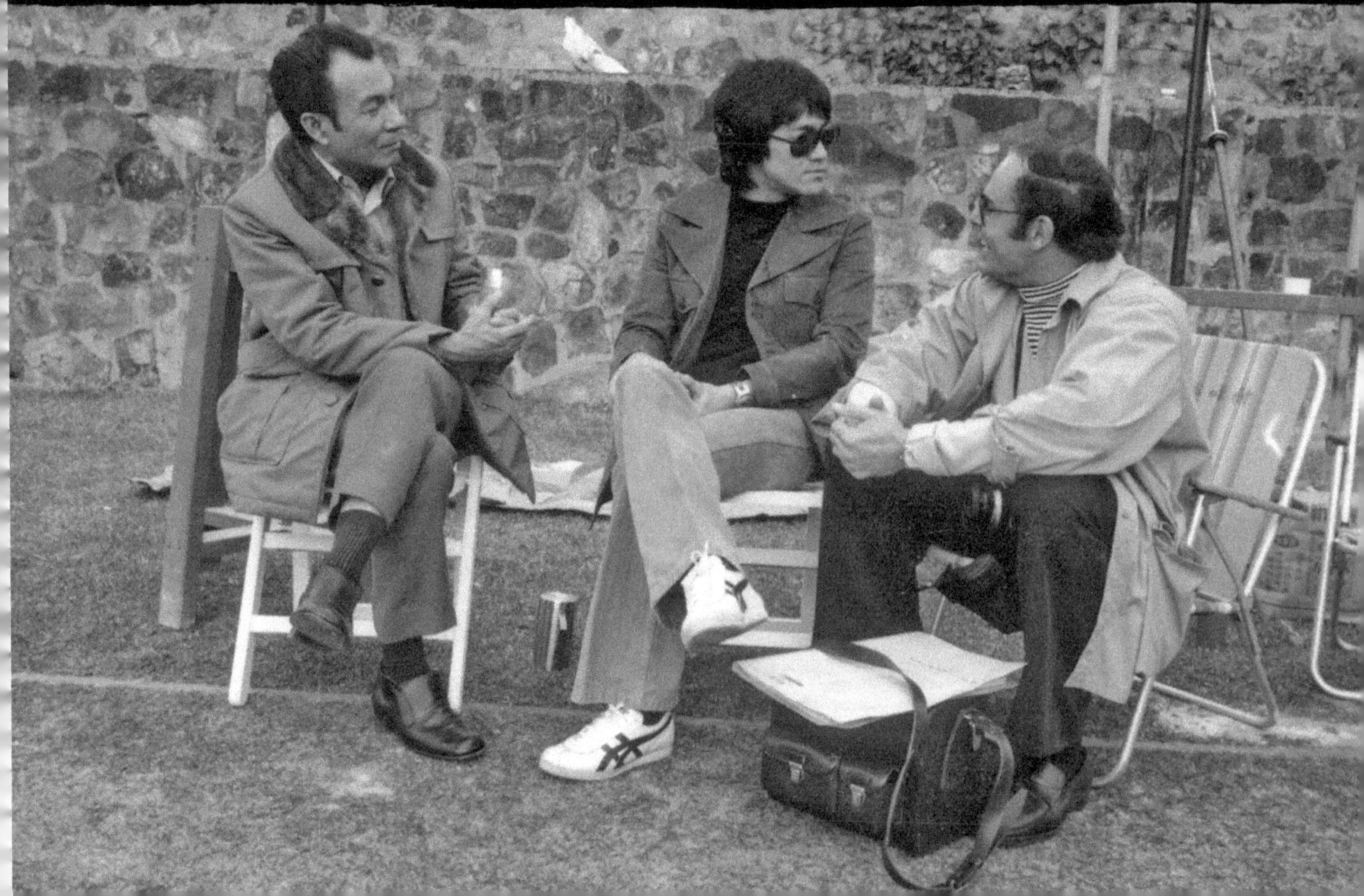

www.ingramcontent.com/pod-product-compliance
Lightning Source LLC
Chambersburg PA
CBHW042034100526
44587CB00029B/4418